WITHDRAWN

Overcoming the Odds

Jim Eisenreich

Bill Gutman

RSVP
RAINTREE
STECK-VAUGHN
PUBLISHERS
The Steck-Vaughn Company

Austin, Texas

Published by Raintree Steck-Vaughn Publishers,
an imprint of Steck-Vaughn Company

Developed for Steck-Vaughn Company by
Visual Education Corporation, Princeton, New Jersey
Project Director: Paula McGuire
Editor: Marilyn Miller
Photo Research: Marty Levick
Electronic Preparation: Cynthia C. Feldner
Production Supervisor: Barbara A. Kopel
Electronic Production: Maxson Crandall, Lisa Evans-Skopas, Christine Osborne
Interior Design: Maxson Crandall

Raintree Steck-Vaughn Publishers staff
Editor: Helene Resky
Project Manager: Joyce Spicer

Photo Credits: Cover and 4: © Rick Stewart/ALLSPORT USA; 7: Rick Stewart/ALLSPORT USA;
11: © Courtesy of St. Cloud Technical High School; 12: © St. Cloud State;
17: © Focus on Sports; 18: © Focus on Sports; 25: © Focus on Sports; 31: © Focus on Sports;
34: © Tom Dipace/Focus on Sports; 36: © AP/Wide World Photos;
37: © Michael Ponzini/Focus on Sports; 39: © Greule Jr./ALLSPORT USA;
41: © Otto Greule Jr./ALLSPORT USA; 42: © Focus on Sports;
43: © 1994 Rosemary Rahn

Library of Congress Cataloging-in-Publication Data
Gutman, Bill.
    Jim Eisenreich/ Bill Gutman.
       p.   cm. — (Overcoming the odds)
    Includes bibliographical references (p.   ) and index.
    Summary: Relates the life story of Jim Eisenreich, a baseball player now with the
Philadelphia Phillies, who has had to contend with Tourette's syndrome but has
continued to play the game he loves.
    ISBN 0-8172-4120-5 (hardcover)
    1. Eisenreich, Jim, 1959– —Juvenile literature.   2. Baseball players—
United States—Biography—Juvenile literature.   3. Tourette syndrome—Patients—
United States—Biography—Juvenile literature.   [1. Eisenreich, Jim, 1959–
2. Baseball players.   3. Tourette syndrome.]   I. Title.   II. Series.
GV865.E43A3 1996
796.357′092—dc20
[B]
                                            95–46206
                                             CIP
                                           AC

Printed and bound in the United States
1 2 3 4 5 6 7 8 9 0 WZ 99 98 97 96 95

Table of Contents

Chapter 1

World Series Star

The setting was the magnificent SkyDome in Toronto, Canada. The event was the second game of the 1993 World Series between the defending champions, the Toronto Blue Jays, and the National League champs, the Philadelphia Phillies. The Blue Jays had won the first game by an 8–5 score. If they won the second, they would take a 2–0 lead in the best-of-seven World Series.

Toronto had big right-hander Dave Stewart on the mound. Stewart was one of baseball's best pitchers in the play-offs and World Series. He had a 10–3 record in six postseasons with the Oakland A's and now the Blue Jays. Philly had star left-hander Terry Mulholland pitching. The Blue Jays were favored to win again on their home field.

The game was scoreless for the first two innings. Then the Phils came to bat in the top of the third. Center fielder Lenny Dykstra opened the inning by drawing a walk. He took second on a wild pitch.

Jim connects for his home run against Toronto's Dave Stewart in the 1993 World Series.

Mariano Duncan drew another walk from Stewart. John Kruk followed with a single to center, scoring Dykstra. Philadelphia had a 1–0 lead.

Then, third baseman Dave Hollins slammed a single to center. Duncan scored with the second run. The Phillies had Stewart on the ropes. A big inning would go a long way toward helping them win the game. The next hitter, Darren Daulton, grounded out to first, but he moved up the runners to second and third.

Now right fielder Jim Eisenreich was up. A base hit would likely score both runners and make it a 4–0 game. Eisenreich was a left-handed hitter who stood straight up at the plate. He was coming off his best season ever, having hit a career-high .318 in 153 games. But he had never been in a pressure spot like this, at least, not in a baseball game.

Stewart stared down from the mound. He wanted to get out of the inning without any more runs being scored. It was one of baseball's classic one-on-one confrontations, just pitcher and hitter. When Stewart got two quick strikes on Eisenreich, the pitcher seemed to be in control.

Now the towering right-hander got set again. The last thing Jim Eisenreich wanted to do was strike out. Even a ground ball might drive in another run. So it was important that he make contact. With the count in his favor, Stewart tried to get Eisenreich to swing at a bad pitch.

He threw a fastball high and inside. But it wasn't quite as high or quite as inside as he wanted it. Jim took a quick step forward with his right foot and whipped the bat around. Jim has a short, quick, compact swing. That makes him normally a line-drive hitter. But this time he hit the ball perfectly.

As Jim ran to first, he watched the ball soar in a deep, high arc toward the right center-field fence. He was just rounding first when the ball passed over the fence for a three-run homer! The blast gave the Phils a commanding 5–0 lead.

Jim's teammates congratulate him after his World Series homer.

When Jim reached the dugout, he was mobbed by his teammates. The Phils went on to win the game 6–4, deadlocking the World Series at one game apiece. Jim's dramatic home run was perhaps the biggest part of the victory.

At the time of his home run, Jim was a 34-year-old veteran. He had come to the majors in 1982. After 11 years, he was finally playing in a World Series. That's every player's dream. But for Jim, hitting that home run was almost secondary to just being there.

Most people never thought Jim Eisenreich would ever be able to complete a full season in the big leagues. Despite being a proven hitter, he played in just 34 games his first year. In his second year, he was in just 2 games, and in his third season, 12 games. After 1984, he didn't appear in the big leagues for nearly three seasons. His comeback from a strange, rare, and sometimes mysterious disorder ranks as one of the most amazing in all of sports.

Chapter 2

A Difficult Childhood

Jim Eisenreich was born in St. Cloud, Minnesota, on April 18, 1959. He was the third of five children born to Cliff and Ann Eisenreich. Jim's father was a schoolteacher who spent many years teaching at a local reform school. His mother was a housewife who worked hard at caring for her large family.

Young Jim seemed perfectly normal in his very early years. He followed his older brothers, Bill and Tom, around, and he liked to play sports. Jim was happy—a typical little boy without a care in the world. But when he was eight years old, everything changed.

This was when Jim began experiencing the first signs that something was wrong. He developed tics. Tics are involuntary muscle contractions, or muscle contractions that a person can't control. Jim would do things like waving his arms, jerking his neck, and contorting his face in different ways. Sometimes the tics were not as bad as at other times. But they never stopped completely.

Jim's parents took him to a doctor. The doctor wasn't sure just what the problem was.

"He put Jim on some medication," said Jim's mother. "I don't even remember what it was. But by sixth grade, Jim was playing hockey. So the doctor said, 'Leave him play. That's all he needs.'"

Jim's parents, however, were still concerned. At one point, his father took him for a psychiatric evaluation. Again, none of the doctors seemed able to diagnose the problem. They simply thought it was some kind of nervous condition that would stop someday.

So Jim continued to play sports, mostly baseball and hockey. His tics also continued. Soon those who knew him well just accepted the tics. Jim was fine in every other way. The movements didn't affect his speech or his ability to do his schoolwork. They didn't affect his play in sports, either. Jim was becoming a fine baseball player who was always the best hitter among his friends. He was already dreaming of someday playing big-league baseball for the home-state Minnesota Twins.

Later, Jim was quoted as saying that he had to endure "torture" in grade school. But as the years went by, he seemed to accept the continuing tics. Jim didn't think of himself as ill or handicapped. Looking back now, though, he admits it wasn't always easy.

"Growing up, they used to tell me I was hyperactive," he recalled. "I had a lot of trouble in school, at church, and later driving a car."

Yet Jim always had many friends. His teammates came to depend on him on the ballfield. By the time

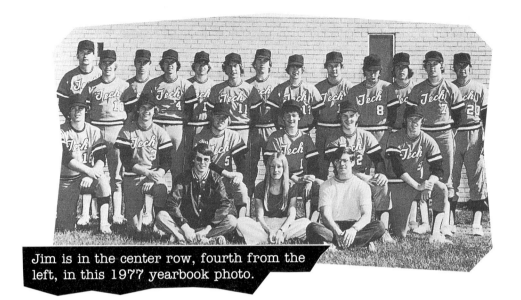

Jim is in the center row, fourth from the left, in this 1977 yearbook photo.

he reached St. Cloud Technical High School, he was already an outstanding baseball player.

Jim's "condition" never caused him to leave a high school baseball game. He also made good grades and graduated with his class in June 1977. That fall, he entered St. Cloud State College, preferring to stay close to home. But always in the back of his mind was the dream of playing in the major leagues.

At St. Cloud State, Jim was an outstanding player who could really hit the ball. His coach, Dennis Lorsung, recalls how Jim's teammates came to accept his tics, movements, and occasional strange sounds.

"Jim was always making some sort of weird noise or movement out there in the field," Lorsung said. "At first, the other outfielders noticed, but after awhile they realized it was just Jim."

Bob Hegman was a teammate of Jim's at St. Cloud State. Hegman later became a scouting and player development administrator with the Kansas City Royals. He, too, remembered Jim at college.

"The same symptoms were always there—the guttural sounds and shakes," Hegman said. "But we just kind of accepted it. This was Jim Eisenreich. And it never affected his baseball. From Little League through college, Jim would hum in the dugout to try to suppress the tics and the twitching. Never did he take himself out of a game, despite the taunts he heard from opposing players and fans."

That was always the difficult part. Some fans and opponents were very mean. They didn't try to understand. They just

Jim was a standout baseball player in high school and college.

saw a ballplayer twitching and shaking and made fun of him. The quiet Eisenreich never said much.

Jim played three years at St. Cloud State and kept improving his game. By this time, he was 5 feet 11 inches tall and weighed about 185 pounds. Jim was a very good outfielder with great speed and a fine throwing arm. But at the plate is where he really excelled. A left-handed hitter, Jim had a beautiful compact swing. He was able to hit line drives to all fields.

After the 1980 college season, Jim received some great news. He had been drafted by the Minnesota Twins on the 16th round of baseball's annual amateur draft. His dream seemed to be coming true.

Chapter 3

The Dream Becomes a Nightmare

Once the Twins picked him, Jim made his decision quickly. He would leave St. Cloud State and sign a professional baseball contract with his home-state team. Things couldn't have worked out better. Twins' scouts saw him as a potentially high-quality big-league hitter. He was just 21 years old. And he was on his way to playing with the Elizabethion club, a low-level minor league team.

Once there, Jim showed the Twins they hadn't made a mistake. He began to hit almost immediately. Jim also played a very solid center field. He still had all of the tics and twitches. But they were no worse than before and didn't really affect his ability to play.

Jim was in 67 games for Elizabethion. He hit .298 with 3 homers and 41 runs batted in. Jim also had 12 doubles, 4 triples, and 12 stolen bases in 15 tries. For his efforts, he was named the league's co-Player of the Year. Near the end of the 1980 season, he moved up to the Class A Wisconsin Rapids in the Midwest League.

Jim played just five games there before the season ended. He hit .438 with 7 hits in 16 at-bats. The Twins then told him he would start the 1981 season with the Wisconsin Rapids. He seemed to be moving along right on schedule. And when the 1981 season started, Jim really began to make his mark.

Jim was driving the ball hard to all fields. He was not a classic slugger with a big swing, but he was slamming line drives over the fences. Jim was already one of the top all-around players in the Midwest League.

Twins' management watched with interest while Jim continued his hard hitting. As the season wore on, they began thinking that they had a future star. Jim seemed to have no weakness at the plate. He was also a fine outfielder. Veteran baseball men watching him felt that he was a natural hitter, the kind that doesn't come along too often.

He proved how good he was all year long. When the 1981 season ended, Jim was second in the league with a .311 batting average. He was also second in the league in RBIs (99), runs scored (101), and total bases. In addition, he led the league in games played (134) and in doubles (27). Jim also had 152 hits and blasted 23 home runs. Because of his great season, he was invited to the Minnesota Twins training camp in 1982.

Now Jim felt he was on the brink of fulfilling his dream. He looked forward to 1982 with great anticipation. The Twins had finished last in the American League's Western Division during the strike-shortened season of 1981. But in 1982 the team promised to have some good young hitters. They included Kent Hrbek, Gary Gaetti, Tom Brunanski, and Gary Ward. This lineup would probably score a lot of runs. It was a great lineup for Jim to join.

During spring training, Jim looked terrific. He was hitting the ball to all fields and making solid contact. To everyone, he looked like a surefire big-league hitter. Not many players make the jump from Class A minor league ball to the majors. They usually play AA and AAA ball first. But Jim made the leap. Shortly before the season began, he was named the Twins' starting center fielder.

Everyone was excited about the potential Jim brought to the club. Owner Calvin Griffith predicted that Jim would "become an All-Star center fielder." Manager Billy Gardner said Jim's presence would mean 10 to 15 extra wins for the team if he played 140 games. There was an awful lot expected of him.

Of course, Jim still had the tics and jerks. Most people assumed they resulted from some kind of nervous condition. As long as they didn't hinder his play, no one really thought much about it. His teammates started calling him "Eisie," and he began hitting just as he had in the minors.

The Twins opened the season at home in the Hubert H. Humphrey Metrodome. Jim hit safely in

Here's Jim getting ready to bat. The Twins first thought he had great potential as both a hitter and an outfielder.

eight of the team's first nine games. On April 16, the Twins left on a ten-game road trip. Jim was already hitting an impressive .344. He seemed to be living up to his preseason potential.

But during the trip, teammates began noticing that his tics and involuntary movements were growing worse. Twins' public relations director Tom Mee remembered attending church with Jim before the last game of the road trip. Both were sitting at the back of the church when Mee noticed something.

"Jim put his head down on the pew in front of us and just started shaking," the public relations director said.

On April 30, the Twins were back home. They were playing the Milwaukee Brewers in front of 23,547 fans at the Metrodome. Jim was still hitting .310, although his hitting had dropped off somewhat

In his first season with the Twins, Jim quickly showed that he was a fine hitter. On April 30, he was hitting .310.

during the road trip. In the sixth inning he was standing out in center field. Manager Gardner noticed that Jim seemed to be taking quick, short, stiff-legged steps between each pitch. He would step first to his left, then to his right. Also, between pitches, Jim was turning his back to the infield. His movements seemed machinelike. When he bent to anticipate the pitch, his body was rigid. It seemed to hinge 90 degrees from the waist.

What they didn't know in the dugout was that Jim was suddenly experiencing terrible symptoms. He began to twitch and shake, almost convulsively. Then his breathing became shallower and faster. He began gasping for air, or hyperventilating. Suddenly, Jim shouted to the umpire to call time out. He then ran off the field into the Minnesota dugout.

In the dugout, the Twins' trainer told Jim to take a drink of water and return to the field. Jim refused. He simply didn't understand what was happening to him. From that point on, Jim's problems became worse.

The same symptoms showed up in each of the next four games. When they appeared, Jim left the game. Then the Twins traveled to Boston. Jim's condition had been reported in the papers there. On May 4, Red Sox fans in the center-field bleachers began getting on him from the first inning.

"What inning are you leaving tonight?" one yelled.

"It's a little cold. And I'm shivering, too!" shouted another one.

"What are you, an epileptic?" a third screamed.

"Shake! Shake! Shake!" others yelled in unison.

The cruel heckling did not let up. Jim had to come out of the game by the third inning. He was still hitting .310 at the time. But the Twins benched him for a couple of games. Then on May 7, before a game in Milwaukee, Jim suddenly ran back into the clubhouse. He started tearing at his clothing and screaming, "I can't breathe!"

At that point, Jim thought he was dying or going insane. He couldn't understand what was happening to him.

"I still don't know what happened," he says, looking back. "It had never been that bad, where I felt I was losing control."

That May 7 Jim left the ballpark and went to the hospital. Teammate Mickey Hatcher spent most of the night with him in the emergency room.

"I just get nervous," Jim said at the time. "When I think about it [the tics, shakes, and hyperventilating] and try to correct it, I make it worse. The more I do it, the madder I get at myself. When I forget about it and have fun, I'm okay."

The team knew it had to take action. Jim was placed on the disabled list. A group of doctors tried to find out just what was wrong. They sent Jim to St. Mary's Hospital in Minneapolis. The doctors there examined Jim and gave him all kinds of tests. Afterward, they still couldn't agree on a diagnosis.

"I've had the problem since I was eight," he said, "but always controlled it before. So I never realized I had such a severe problem. When I was finally placed on the disabled list and hospitalized, I was relieved. I thought, 'At last, someone is going to help me.'"

But it was easier said than done. Doctors came away from the exam with three possible diagnoses. The first two were psychological disorders. One possibility was that Jim had a form of performance anxiety caused by a fear of failure. A common name for it is stage fright. In other words, Jim was so frightened of failing on the field that his symptoms became uncontrollable.

The second possibility was something called agoraphobia. Agoraphobia is a fear of being in open or public places.

The third possibility seemed stranger yet. It was something called Tourette's syndrome. The Twins' doctors simply didn't believe this was the cause. Jim listened, and his desperation grew. Was his baseball career over almost before it had started?

Chapter 4

Out of Baseball Forever?

In trying to understand Jim's problem, the Twins' doctors had to first eliminate agoraphobia as the cause. Jim had never had a problem hitting or fielding in the minor leagues. The doctors reasoned that if he had a fear of being in open or public places, his symptoms would have first appeared in the minors.

The Twins' doctors felt that performance anxiety was a much more likely possibility. In the majors, Jim had been booed and heckled from the outfield bleachers. The Twins' organization believed that this behavior by the fans brought Jim's stage fright out in the open.

One reason the Twins' doctors didn't think much about Tourette's syndrome was that it was far more difficult to diagnose. Tourette's syndrome is an illness that still isn't completely understood. It is certain, however, that Tourette's syndrome is not a psychological problem, like stage fright. Tourette's syndrome is a physiological disorder. That means it is caused by a problem within the body not the mind.

Tourette's syndrome was named for a French doctor, Gilles de la Tourette. He first identified the disease in 1885. The cause remains unknown. However, the problem is now considered to be neuro-chemical. In other words, somewhere in the brain a chemical may be released abnormally, triggering the symptoms. Or, perhaps signals from one nerve to another are not processed correctly.

The symptoms are very real. People suffering from Tourette's syndrome often must live with symptoms that can be humiliating and sometimes violent. These people may have tics and muscle contractions that they cannot predict or control. Also, some suffer from a tendency to make involuntary sounds like grunting, snorting, or barking. Sometimes they shout obscenities, words they wouldn't use if they could control themselves. Jim sometimes made guttural sounds, though he did not say obscenities.

Dr. Frank Abuzzahab was the expert on Tourette's syndrome at St. Mary's Hospital. He believed that Jim had the disorder. But the Twins' team doctors continued to argue that Jim's problem was a kind of stage fright brought on by large crowds. One described Jim as having "double-deck syndrome."

Later, Dr. Arthur Shapiro, director of the Tourette and Tic Laboratory and Clinic of the Mount Sinai School of Medicine in New York, supported Dr. Abuzzahab's diagnosis. Said Dr. Shapiro, "If

Dr. Abuzzahab diagnosed him as having Tourette, he probably has it."

But the Twins' doctors still refused to accept the diagnosis. They began giving Jim different medications to help him overcome what they believed was stage fright. Jim took the medications for just a couple of days and said they didn't work.

Jim felt all along that he probably had Tourette's syndrome. He thought the reported symptoms of the illness matched his perfectly.

"They [the Twins' doctors] were giving me tests for mental competency," he said. "They weren't giving me physical tests. I wanted to see what my body was doing."

But the doctors treating him still rejected the possibility of Tourette's syndrome. They felt that his breathing attacks, or hyperventilation, and his tics were unrelated.

Jim returned to the lineup briefly several weeks after being placed on the disabled list. The first couple of games back he felt all right. But he was being given two powerful tranquilizers. The problem was that they made him drowsy.

"I was beat, physically tired," he remembered. "I was taking a lot of medication."

The manager and other baseball people felt it was dangerous to send a player taking those drugs up to the plate to face a 90-mile-per-hour fastball. He might not have the reflexes to duck if a bad pitch was coming at his head. In mid-June, Jim was placed on the disabled list once again. His season was basically over.

Jim played in only 34 games in 1982. Despite his problems, he still managed a .303 batting average. That showed what a fine natural hitter he was. Among his hits were six doubles and a pair of home runs. He also had nine runs batted in. He struck out just

Jim began showing terrible symptoms when he was playing for the Twins. He didn't know what was happening to him.

13 times in 99 at-bats. But Jim's problems continued. His future in baseball was seriously in doubt. Even during the off-season, the problems did not disappear.

"I tried to go out to do a little hunting with my brother," Jim said. "He drove and I sat in the back-seat because of the spells. When we finally got where we were going and started to scout out the area for deer, I only got about 200 yards before I was wrecked. We just turned and came back home."

Jim began spending a great deal of time alone, often in the basement of his parents' home.

"I stayed by myself because I was embarrassed," he said.

Spring training for the 1983 season rolled around. Jim was there to try again. He was still try-ing different medications. Most of them were tran-quilizers. He hoped they would calm him down enough to play without the kinds of attacks he had had the last year.

Once again he looked great in spring training. He batted .400 during exhibition games. But when the season started, the same things happened. Jim felt he couldn't go through all of it again. So, after just two games, he decided to leave the team. The Twins then put Jim on the voluntary retired list. He didn't play again the rest of the season.

At this point the team sent Jim to a hypnotist, who tried to help him by using posthypnotic sugges-tion. The hypnotist repeated over and over again to

Jim that he would play well and feel good about it. He told Jim to concentrate more on the game than on the crowd.

Back home, Jim played ball for the local amateur team, the St. Cloud Saints. He was the team's star, hitting over .500. The team won the Minnesota amateur championship. It wasn't the big leagues. But surrounded by friends and family, Jim had an enjoyable time.

"It was baseball," he said. "That was the main thing. And I got to play with my younger brother, Charlie, which was always a dream."

But the big-league dream was still with Jim. He returned to the Twins to try once again in 1984. This time Jim started the exhibition season with eight straight hits. But no one got excited because of what had happened the past two seasons.

After that, Jim began to struggle. His symptoms were still there. And now he also wasn't hitting. He had a sore elbow, and the club began using him more as a designated hitter. That way, he wouldn't have to play in the field. As the regular season neared, the team felt that Jim might finally have things under control.

"He looks the best I've seen him in two years," said manager Billy Gardner. "He's enjoying himself. He's much more relaxed."

Jim tried to keep the pressure off. He decided not to talk to reporters. Everyone was pulling for him to make it. Unfortunately, things didn't work out with the Twins once again. Jim had continued to take a combination of drugs used to treat Tourette's syndrome. The medication had stopped his hyperventilating, but it made him drowsy. The drugs had been prescribed by a hometown doctor. The Twins' medical staff no longer wanted him on these medications. They had made Jim so drowsy that he had fallen asleep during team meetings. The Twins finally told him to stop the drugs and accept their treatment for agoraphobia or else go down to the minor leagues. Jim refused the demotion. But he admitted he was still taking the medication.

"I never want to hyperventilate again," he told the Twins' organization.

On June 4, 1984, Jim was placed on the voluntary retired list. He had played in just 12 games in the 1984 season. And for the first time he didn't hit well. He batted .219, getting just 7 hits in 32 at-bats. When he returned to St. Cloud, it looked as if his major league career was definitely over.

Chapter 5

Another Chance

Jim was just 25 years old. Nearly all his life he had wanted to be a big-league ballplayer. Now, because of this still-mysterious illness, the dream had become a nightmare. The easy way would have been to accept defeat and stay in St. Cloud. But that was not Jim's style. Like most fine athletes, he had a special will to win. That meant winning the battle against the enemy that had defeated him since 1982—Tourette's syndrome.

By this time, Jim and the doctors he had consulted on his own were convinced that his problem was Tourette's syndrome. It was now a matter of getting it under control. They had to search for the right amount of medication. To help them, Jim had to learn to identify the kinds of situations that made his symptoms get out of control. He was still taking a tranquilizer. But he was trying to limit the amounts so he would not become drowsy.

Once again he played baseball with the St. Cloud Saints. He stayed close to home, seeing only family and old friends. Slowly, he reduced the amount of medication he was taking. He batted .542 for the St. Cloud team in 1985. There was still very little doubt about his ability as a hitter. There was also no doubt that Jim still enjoyed baseball immensely. In the back of his mind, he began thinking about trying to play professionally one more time.

Jim contacted the Twins. He said he might like to come to spring training again in 1986. But General Manager Andy MacPhail told him straight out, "The truth is we're not going to let you play."

Jim waited another year, playing again at home for his amateur team. Then in 1986, he contacted Bob Hegman, his former teammate years earlier at St. Cloud State. Hegman was now the Kansas City Royals' administrative assistant of scouting and player development. He knew Jim's background and was aware of his situation as well as anyone. Jim said that he wanted to try to make the majors again. He asked if Hegman thought the Royals might be interested.

Hegman believed Jim when he said he hadn't hyperventilated in two years. He convinced Royals' general manager John Schuerholz that Jim was worth the gamble. The Royals claimed Jim from the Twins for the waiver price of one dollar. A team that has rights to a player they no longer want may put him on waivers. If no one claims him, they will usually give him his release. It's just a formality. That's why the price was so low.

"I called Jim myself," Hegman said, "and told him, 'I thought you were worth a dollar.'"

But the Royals did have a concern. They knew that Jim's medication could make him groggy. It could cut his reaction time at the plate. This was something the Twins had also worried about.

"We had to know about the medication," Hegman said. "Jim told me, 'I take so little of it now that it's not a problem.' Then I told him, 'Let's go get 'em.'"

So in March 1987, Jim Eisenreich was once again in Florida at a major league spring training baseball camp. He showed very quickly that he could still hit major league pitching. People who knew him well, like his boyhood pal Jay Johnson, saw a change at this time.

"Jim became much more self-confident in 1987," Johnson recalled. "Before, when he was playing at home with St. Cloud, he wouldn't talk to the press. They would wait outside our

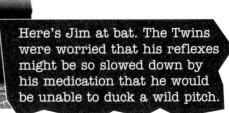

Here's Jim at bat. The Twins were worried that his reflexes might be so slowed down by his medication that he would be unable to duck a wild pitch.

bus when we'd travel to games, and I'd ask Jim if he wanted to talk to them. He always said 'no.' Now he's talking again."

In fact, Jim was saying "yes" nearly every time someone requested an interview. He also appeared twice on national television.

"I just decided I had to talk to the press," Jim said. "It's better they should hear it from me."

Jim also agreed to serve as a spokesman for the Tourette's Syndrome Association. He knew he would be even more effective if he made it all the way back. So when the Royals asked him to start the season playing for the minor league Class AA Memphis Chicks, Jim agreed immediately. Once there, he began to hit at nearly a .400 clip. Everyone in the Royals' organization was impressed.

"We plan to give Jim a chance with the Royals before the season is complete," General Manager Schuerholz explained. "We want to be certain that it is the right time, right move, and not disruptive for anyone."

In Memphis, Jim was used as a designated hitter. That meant he didn't have to play in the outfield. The team said the reason was because he had strained his elbow throwing a wet ball in spring training. Others felt the team was simply trying to protect him. After all, he had never had a problem at the plate. His problems always surfaced while he was in the outfield.

There was little doubt about what Jim was able to do with the bat. By the second week in June, he was leading the Southern League in hitting with a .379 average.

"He's the same kind of hitter as Don Mattingly," said Memphis manager Bob Schaefer. Mattingly, who plays for the New York Yankees, was one of the best hitters in the majors at the time.

That was a supreme compliment. But Jim knew he had a long way to go. Though he roomed with first baseman Matt Winters, Jim kept to himself quite often. Occasionally, he went with some teammates to wrestling matches. But he was still concerned about his health and keeping himself on an even keel.

"I feel fine right now," Jim said. "My problem is under control. I've survived it all so far."

Surviving it all wasn't easy. For the past five years, Jim had undergone every kind of test, both physical and psychological. He'd had to take a variety of medications before doctors discovered the best one for him. He'd had to listen to the taunts of fans. He'd had to read stories about himself that were all wrong. And many people still simply didn't understand his illness.

One of his close friends, Jay Johnson, said, "He went through more hell in a couple of years than anyone should have to go through in a lifetime."

But Jim's desire to try it again finally paid off. On June 17, it was announced that the Royals had

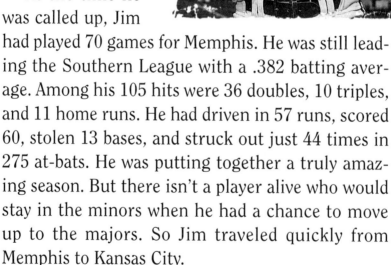

A great moment in Jim's life was when he returned to the majors as a member of the Kansas City Royals. Jim's courage and determination made his comeback possible.

purchased his contract from Memphis. Jim was on his way to the big leagues once again. It was an incredible comeback.

At the time he was called up, Jim had played 70 games for Memphis. He was still leading the Southern League with a .382 batting average. Among his 105 hits were 36 doubles, 10 triples, and 11 home runs. He had driven in 57 runs, scored 60, stolen 13 bases, and struck out just 44 times in 275 at-bats. He was putting together a truly amazing season. But there isn't a player alive who would stay in the minors when he had a chance to move up to the majors. So Jim traveled quickly from Memphis to Kansas City.

In doing so, he had defied the odds. In 1984, he had left the Twins after just 12 games. It looked to everyone as if his major league career was over. Now, three years later, he was back. He wanted to make sure that he stayed.

Chapter 6

A Solid Big-Leaguer at Last

This is not a story with a fairy-tale ending. Jim didn't return to the Royals and become an instant superstar. It was just amazing in itself that he was there. Now he had to contribute.

In 1987, the Royals were in a tight divisional race with Minnesota and Oakland. The team had a solid starting outfield consisting of Bo Jackson, Willie Wilson, and Danny Tartabull. Jim's role would be to serve as a left-handed designated hitter (DH) and also as a pinch hitter.

That's what he did for the remainder of the season. He spent two weeks on the disabled list with a strained elbow from August 25 to September 9. Otherwise, he was limited to being a designated hitter and pinch hitter. He didn't play a single game in the outfield.

When it ended, the Royals were second to the Twins in the American League West. Jim batted just .238 in 44 games, getting 25 hits in just 105 at-bats. He had 8 doubles, 2 triples, 4 homers, and 21 runs batted in. But considering what he had been through and that he hadn't seen big-league pitching in three years, his comeback was more than a success.

And his Tourette's syndrome remained under control. He still had some tics and involuntary movements. He would always have them. But they didn't keep him from playing. And when he returned for the 1988 season, he made the Royals' opening-day roster.

On April 6, Jim made his first appearance in a big-league outfield since the 1984 season. He had no problems. This was the last barrier he had to cross. Now he could concentrate on just being a ballplayer. That was what he had wanted all along.

The problem in 1988 was an old-fashioned batting slump. Jim just couldn't seem to get in a good groove at the plate. It is something nearly every player goes through at some time. Finally, in early July, the Royals felt that Jim needed to be playing every day to regain his

In the 1988 season, Jim first began playing outfield for the Royals. This was the final obstacle he had to overcome. Now he could simply be a regular ballplayer. Here he is about to make a great catch of a ball hit by Yankee Jesse Barfield.

usually reliable batting stroke. They optioned him to Omaha, the Royals' Class AAA minor league team in Nebraska.

Jim took the demotion well. He played in 36 games for Omaha, hitting .298. On August 12, after about five weeks in the minors, Jim was brought back to Kansas City. He then began to hit like everyone knew he could. From August 12 to the end of the year, he banged away at a .271 clip.

That gave him just a .218 average for the year in 82 games. He had just 1 homer and 19 runs batted in. At the plate, it was his poorest season in the majors. But in another way, it had to be his greatest. That's because Jim played 64 games in the outfield. He showed no recurrence of the terrible symptoms he had had with the Twins. Now he felt he was all the way back.

So in 1989, Jim Eisenreich could finally relax completely and simply be a ballplayer. No one worried about his health or his medication. Tourette's syndrome never goes away completely. But Jim now had it under control. He proved it by producing his best season to date.

The Royals had a fine team in 1989. George Brett, Willie Wilson, Danny Tartabull, Bob Boone, Frank White, and Bo Jackson were all outstanding players. Bret Saberhagen, Mark Gubicza, and Tom Gordon were a solid trio of pitchers. The team was in a divisional race with Oakland and California. And Jim Eisenreich was in the thick of things from the start.

It turned out that Oakland had too much firepower and won 99 games to take the American League West. Kansas City finished second, 7 games behind with a 92–70 record. Jim played an important role all year long. He missed a little over two weeks in late August and early September with a pulled hamstring muscle. Otherwise, he saw a lot of action.

Playing in 134 games, Jim hit a solid .293. Of his 139 hits, 33 were doubles, and 7 were triples. He had 9 homers and 59 RBIs. In addition, he had a career best—27 stolen bases, ninth in the league. Playing a lot of right field, Jim led the team's outfielders in putouts. He was doing it all.

In fact, Jim led the Royals in batting average, doubles, and steals. He had a 13-game hitting streak in June. In both May and August, Jim was the Royals' Player of the Month. He also belted his first career grand-slam homer, connecting off star left-hander Randy Johnson of Seattle. When the season ended, Jim was named Royals' Player of the Year.

It was more of the same for the next two seasons. Jim hit .280 in 1990 and .301 in 1991. In 1990 he had

Jim is a multitalented player. Besides having great hitting and fielding skills, he is an excellent base runner.

496 at-bats in 142 games. The next year he was credited with 375 at-bats. He played nearly every day and was a valuable left-handed batter to have in the lineup. Jim had become a solid major league player.

His life had also changed in other ways. With his illness identified and under control, Jim was more open. In 1990, he married Leann Danner. Then in January 1991, he was chosen to receive the first Tony Conigliaro Award. This award is presented to the major league player who "has overcome adversity through the attributes of spirit, determination, and courage." These were qualities exhibited by the late Boston Red Sox star Tony Conigliaro. Conigliaro had returned to the majors after a serious eye injury caused when he was hit by a wild pitch.

There was another important event in Jim and Leann's lives in 1991. On May 26, their daughter, Lauren, was born. Jim's life had really turned around. Those who knew how much he had gone through felt no one deserved it more.

Chapter 7

The Phillies and the World Series

Jim tested the free-agent market before the 1992 season. But instead of changing teams, he signed again with the Royals. His playing time was cut somewhat that year. He appeared in just 113 games and hit .269, his lowest average since 1988. Yet he still had real value as a ballplayer.

Jim was the American League's top pinch hitter. He got 10 pinch hits in 27 at-bats for a .370 average. Pinch-hitting isn't easy, because a player has to come to bat cold after sitting in the dugout most of the game. Jim also committed just one error in the 88 games he played in the field. In addition, he continued to hit well late in the season. His career average for the month of August was .346.

But after the season, Jim again began thinking about a change. Once more a free agent, he could sign with any team that wanted him. On January 19, he surprised people by signing with the Philadelphia Phillies of the National League. That, in itself, showed how much his confidence had grown. Jim wasn't worried about going to a new city and a new league.

This was a tough and talented Philadelphia team. The Phillies had many ballplayers who played hard every game. The team was led by center fielder Lenny Dykstra, first baseman John Kruk, catcher Darren Daulton, and third baseman Dave Hollins. Pitchers Terry Mulholland, Curt Schilling, and Mitch "Wild Thing" Williams anchored the mound staff.

Jim played right field against right-handed pitching and also pinch-hit. With the Phillies winning the National League's Eastern Division, Jim put together perhaps his finest season ever. He did it at age 34, a time when many players are slowing down.

Jim appeared in a career-high 153 games and batted a career-best .318. Among his 115 hits were 17 doubles, 4 triples, and 7 home runs. He also had 54 runs batted in. Again Jim showed his fine batting eye by striking out only 36 times in 362 at-bats. He was one of the Phils' most solid players.

Jim didn't hit well (2 for 15) in the National League Championship Series. But the Phils defeated the favored Atlanta Braves, four games to two. Now they were in the World Series against Toronto.

Toronto won the World Series in six games (4–2) to repeat as world champs. But it was Jim who hit that dramatic three-run homer off Dave Stewart in the second game to help bring his team even.

Jim wound up hitting just .231 in the World Series. But he started all six games, getting 9 hits in 26 trips to the plate and driving in 7 runs. As usual, he hit well when it counted. Although his team lost, playing in the World Series was something that meant a great deal to Jim. It was almost as if it helped to make up for the problems he had had early in his career.

There were more ups in 1994. The best was probably the birth of his son, Tyler James, on March 22. Jim batted an even .300 in 104 games. He drove

home 43 runs with his 87 hits. The season ended on August 12, when the players' union called for a strike, in a labor dispute with the owners.

Jim Eisenreich was 36 years old early in the 1995 season. Most ballplayers are retired by age 40. But Jim has not only been playing, he has

Jim had no problems playing right field for the Phillies against right-handed pitchers.

Here's Jim's daughter, Lauren, holding his bat. His wife Leann holds their son, Tyler James, who was born in 1994.

been playing the best baseball of his life. Jim has earned the respect of his opponents as well as his teammates.

Jim also feels a responsibility to others. He knows that with a little less will to triumph, he could have spent his life hiding in St. Cloud.

"I would like kids to look at me as a positive role model," he said. "Not only kids with Tourette's syndrome, but any kids."

Jim Eisenreich has overcome a very strange and frightening illness to become a husband, father, and star athlete. He also enjoys hunting, fishing, and golf. And he makes time for children with Tourette's syndrome and their families. Jim knows just how important it is to have people believe in you.

Jim Eisenreich's
Career Highlights

1980 Selected by Minnesota Twins in 16th round of June 1980 draft.

1982 Opens season as Twins starting center fielder. Hits safely in eight of team's first nine games. On disabled list with neurological movement disorder (Tourette's syndrome). Season ends after 34 games.

1986 Claimed on waivers by Kansas City Royals after being out of professional baseball since June 4, 1984.

1987 Returns to major leagues with Royals. Leads American League with three pinch-hit doubles for the season.

1988 Makes appearance in the outfield on April 6, his first since 1984.

1989 Hits first career grand-slam home run off Randy Johnson of Seattle on August 19. Has 13-game hitting streak from June 11 to June 24. Leads Royals in batting average, doubles, and stolen bases. Named Royals' Player of the Year.

1990 Ties club record with three doubles in New York on May 18. Has 11-game hitting streak from July 30 to August 12.

1991 Has career-high .301 batting average. Ties club record with three doubles against New York on April 13. Has 12-game hitting streak from April 20 to May 3. Named first-ever winner of Tony Conigliaro Award, given to the major league player who has overcome adversity through the attributes of spirit, determination, and courage.

1992 Is American League's top pinch hitter with a .370 average (10 for 27). Commits just one error in 88 games.

1993 Has career-best .318 batting average. Hits three-run homer off Toronto's Dave Stewart in second game of the World Series.

1994 Hits .300 or better for third time in last four seasons. Raises his career batting average to a very solid .285.

Jim Eisenreich's Major League Career Record

Year	Team	G	BA	AB	R	H	2B	3B	HR	RBI
1982	Minnesota	34	.303	99	10	30	6	0	2	9
1983	Minnesota	2	.286	7	1	2	1	0	0	0
1984	Minnesota	12	.219	32	1	7	1	0	0	3
1985	did not play—illness									
1986	did not play—illness									
1987	Kansas City	44	.238	105	10	25	8	2	4	21
1988	Kansas City	82	.218	202	26	44	8	1	1	19
1989	Kansas City	134	.293	475	64	139	33	7	9	59
1990	Kansas City	142	.280	496	61	139	29	7	5	51
1991	Kansas City	135	.301	375	47	113	22	3	2	47
1992	Kansas City	113	.269	353	31	95	13	3	2	28
1993	Philadelphia	153	.318	362	51	115	17	4	7	54
1994	Philadelphia	104	.300	290	42	87	15	4	4	43
Major League Totals		**955**	**.285**	**2,796**	**344**	**796**	**153**	**31**	**36**	**334**

Jim Eisenreich's Postseason Record

League Championship Series Record

Year	Team	G	BA	AB	R	H	2B	3B	HR	RBI
1993	Philadelphia	6	.133	15	0	2	1	0	0	1

World Series Record

Year	Team	G	BA	AB	R	H	2B	3B	HR	RBI
1993	Philadelphia	6	.231	26	3	9	0	0	1	7

Further Reading

Carroll, Bob. *The Major League Way to Play Baseball.* New York: Simon & Schuster, 1991.

Duden, Jane. *Baseball.* New York: Macmillan Child Group, 1991.

Gutman, Bill. *Baseball.* North Vancouver, BC, Canada: Marshall Cavendish, 1990.

Palmer, Pete and Thom, John, eds. *The Baseball Record Book.* New York: Simon and Schuster Trade, 1991.

Tierstein, Mark Alan. *Baseball.* Austin, TX: Raintree Steck-Vaughn, 1994.

Weiner, Eric. *The Kids' Complete Baseball Catalogue.* New York: Simon and Schuster Trade, 1990.

Index

Index cont.